STICK

Glue Yourself to Godly Friends

Kevin Johnson

DEEPER SERIES

STICK

Glue Yourself to Godly Friends

Kevin Johnson

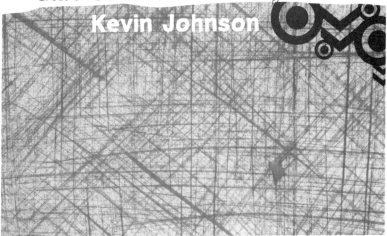

ZONDERVAN®

ZONDERVAN.com/
AUTHORTRACKER
follow your favorite authors

youth
specialties

**youth
specialties**

Stick: Glue Yourself to Godly Friends
Copyright 2007 by Kevin Johnson

Youth Specialties resources, 300 S. Pierce St., El Cajon, CA 92020 are published by
Zondervan, 5300 Patterson Ave. SE, Grand Rapids, MI 49530.

Library of Congress Cataloging-in-Publication Data

Johnson, Kevin (Kevin Walter)
  Stick : glue yourself to godly friends / by Kevin Johnson.
    p. cm.
  ISBN-10: 0-310-27490-7 (pbk.)
  ISBN-13: 978-0-310-27490-2 (pbk.)
  1. Friendship—Biblical teaching—Juvenile literature. I. Title.
  BS2545.F75J64 2007
  241'.6762—dc22

2007039353

Web site addresses listed in this book were current at the time of publication. Please
contact Youth Specialties via e-mail (YS@YouthSpecialties.com) to report URLs that
are no longer operational and replacement URLs if available.

Cover and interior design by SharpSeven Design

Printed in the United States of America

---

08 09 10 11 12 • 20 19 18 17 16 15 14 13 12 11 10 9 8 7 6 5 4 3 2

Contents

Start here

It's cool that you're cracking open this book. If you've ever wanted to dig into the Bible or find out what it takes to grow in your faith, the DEEPER series is like an enormous neon finger that'll point you toward exactly what you need to know.

Stick contains 20 Bible studies that build piece by piece. You'll check out Scripture, think for yourself, and feed on insights you might not otherwise find. In the process you'll discover the amazing friends God has in store for you—people who will care for you and stick by you forever. And you'll get the big message—that you need those friends to help you follow Jesus.

Don't rush. Pick your own pace—from a study a day to a study a week. Actually, the slower you go, the more you'll gain. While each study is just a couple pages long, every one of them is tagged with another page of bonus material that can help you dig even deeper.

Each study opens with a mostly blank page featuring a single Bible verse that sums up the main point. These verses are worth memorizing, just as a way to grasp the awesome truths of God's Word. Then comes **START**, a brief introduction to get your brain geared up for the topic. **READ** takes you to a short Scripture passage. You can either read it here in the book or grab your own Bible and read the passage there. **THINK** helps you examine the main ideas of the passage, and **LIVE** makes it easy to apply what you learn. Finally, **WRAP** pulls everything together.

Then there's that bonus material. **MORE THOUGHTS TO MULL** tosses you a few more questions to ask yourself or others, and **MORE SCRIPTURES TO DIG** leads you to related Bible passages to give you the full scoop on a topic.

Whether you read on your own or get together with a group, *Stick* will help you take your next step in becoming wildly devoted to Jesus. If you're ready to grab hold of a heart-to-heart, all-out relationship with God, dig in!

1. GET IN THE FLOW

Real love starts and ends with God

1 John 4:7

Dear friends, let us love one another, for love comes from God.

Everyone who loves has been born of God and knows God.

➔   **START** You could plow a canoe upstream to the start of the Mississippi River in northern Minnesota, a drip of water almost narrow enough to hop across. Then you could powerboat 2,320 miles southward to dangle your toes in the 300 trillion gallons of water that spill from that river each day into the Gulf of Mexico. Finally, you could leap overboard and let that immense flow flush you out to sea. But you still wouldn't experience a force as massive as God's love. It's mightier than anything on earth.

God loves you enormously. How much does that fact matter to you—a lot, a little, or not at all? Why?

➔   **READ** 1 John 4:7-12, 19-21

⁷Dear friends, let us love one another, for love comes from God. Everyone who loves has been born of God and knows God. ⁸Whoever does not love does not know God, because God is love. ⁹This is how God showed his love among us: He sent his one and only Son into the world that we might live through him. ¹⁰This is love: not that we loved God, but that he loved us and sent his Son as an atoning sacrifice for our sins. ¹¹Dear friends, since God so loved us, we also ought to love one another. ¹²No one has ever seen God; but if we love one another, God lives in us and his love is made complete in us...

¹⁹We love because he first loved us. ²⁰If we say we love God yet hate a brother or sister, we are liars. For if we do not love a fellow believer, whom we have seen, we cannot love God, whom we have not seen. ²¹And he has given us this command: Those who love God must also love one another.

➔ **THINK** How does God prove he cares for you?

Atonement means making amends for doing wrong. So when verse 10 speaks of an "atoning sacrifice," it's referring to the death of God's Son— Jesus—on the cross. Jesus' death paid the penalty for your sins, making a way for you to live tight with God as your Friend and Master, now and forever (Romans 6:23). Proof of God's love doesn't get any bigger than that.

The death of Jesus says everything about God's love for you. So what does your love for people—or lack of it—say about your devotion to God?

You can't read that passage and miss God's repeated command to love others. But answer this: Where can you get the power to pull that off?

➔ **LIVE** When has God's love seemed most real to you?

When you trust the fact that Jesus lived, died, and rose for you, you dive into the mighty flow of God's love. And when you love others and let them love you, you feel a raging surge of God's care. His love is "made complete" in you (verse 12).

So God's love is supposed to flow *to* you—then *through* you to others. How are you doing at getting God's love—and giving it away?

➔ **WRAP** Love begins and ends with God. So if you want to figure out what true love looks like, get to know God. If you want to really care for friends, first plunge into the mighty stream of God's love. And if you want God's care for you to feel unmistakably real, stick tight to people who strive to love all-out like he does.

» MORE THOUGHTS TO MULL

- Who in your life has showered you with God's care? What did they do—and not do?

- How much of God's love can you experience if you cut yourself off from other people?

- How would you answer a girl who says she's never really felt loved? Or a guy who tells you no one has ever really cared about him?

» MORE SCRIPTURES TO DIG

- The message of God's love winds through the Bible like a river, growing continually from the first page to the last. One crucial verse along the way is **Romans 5:8**. It says that even though we don't deserve God's kindness, God loves us anyway. We were sinners who snubbed him, yet God still sent Jesus to die for us.

- Fun doesn't get much more intense than sitting under a body-thumping waterfall. And **Ephesians 3:14-21** is like climbing into the turbo-rushing waters of God's love. The apostle Paul's prayer for his close friends in the ancient city of Ephesus packs a powerful point: God wants us to experience the flood of his overwhelming love.

- There are loads of things that make it tough to feel God's care. Yet **Romans 8:38-39** says there's nothing that can halt the flow of God's love in your life.

- The Bible never splits up love for God and love for people—you can't have one without the other. Check **Matthew 22:34-40** for the "Great Commandment," where Jesus tells you to put God at the top of your list of important things in life—and to rank people a close second.

2. YOUR PLACE AT THE PARTY

God is putting together a people

Titus 2:14 (NLT)

He gave his life to free us from every kind of sin, to cleanse us, and to make us his very own people, totally committed to doing good deeds.

➜ **START** If God ever dozed off, here's what he might dream: *a boundless swarm of people...not just strangers jostling randomly like in a mall, but a mass tightly bonded to him and to each other...the group's cool vibe pulls in more and more people...the throng loves the party so much, they decide to stick together for eternity.* Now that's a dream that would shake God awake. He'd slap his forehead and congratulate himself for one of the greatest ideas ever to pop forth from the divine mind.

Get this: That crowd is absolutely real. It's a get-together of God's people that starts now and lasts forever in heaven. So if God offered you an all-access pass to his bash, would you take it? Why—or why not?

➜ **READ** Titus 2:11-14 (NLT)

> [11]For the grace of God has been revealed, bringing salvation to all people. [12]And we are instructed to turn from godless living and sinful pleasures. We should live in this evil world with wisdom, righteousness, and devotion to God, [13]while we look forward with hope to that wonderful day when the glory of our great God and Savior, Jesus Christ, will be revealed. [14]He gave his life to free us from every kind of sin, to cleanse us, and to make us his very own people, totally committed to doing good deeds.

➜ **THINK** That dense passage finishes with the gigantic point that God aims to build a one-of-a-kind people. But notice that God's plan starts with "grace," the undeserved kindness he pours out on you and the rest of the human race. And "salvation" sums up everything God does to rescue you from sin and build a relationship with you.

So what does God's grace train you to do?

I can say "no" to...   I can say "yes" to a life that is...

Check out the meaning of some other words in this passage: "godless living" is the ugly attitude that says God doesn't matter in life, and the evil actions we're capable of when we ignore God and his commands. "Sinful pleasures" are cravings to do wrong. God wants you to live with "wisdom" (you act rightly toward yourself), "righteousness" (toward others), and "devotion" (toward him).

Look at verse 14. Exactly what kind of group does God intend to create?

➜   **LIVE** Why do you think God wants to make a group that's big on love and eager to get along with him and with each other?

Imagine a cage packed full of people battling one another for survival and locked in a fight to the death. Got the picture? That's the total opposite of the loving, peaceful place God aims to create. John 1:12 says that when you believe in Jesus, you become a child of God. You accept his love. You have a home in heaven. But it's not just you and Jesus jammin' together. He plans for all his children to stick tight as "a chosen people, a royal priesthood, a holy nation, God's special possession" (1 Peter 2:9).

What sounds good or bad about being part of God's people?

How ready are you for God to teach you how to be an amazing friend to everyone on earth—and in heaven?

➜   **WRAP** God has a spot for you in his party, a bash that rocks with the rhythm of God's love. There's no better place to be. And if you stick tight with God's people, the fun starts now.

❱❱   MORE THOUGHTS TO MULL

- When have you felt connected to other Christians? What makes you feel detached?

- Do you know someone who's totally into growing closer to God? How much do you want someone like that as a close friend? What might hold you back from having a friendship with someone like that?

- How does God's grace—the kindness God offers that you don't deserve—make you want to say *no* to doing wrong?

» MORE SCRIPTURES TO DIG

- You don't have to convince God to let you into his heavenly party. It's not about whether you're good enough. Getting in is all about Jesus. When you trust Jesus—that is, when you accept who he is and what he's done for you—you change from being God's enemy to being God's friend. You can spot that fact in **Colossians 1:21-23**, which sums up what Jesus has done to straighten out our relationship with God. People have a *problem*—sin (verse 21). God has a *solution*—Jesus (verse 22). And God requires a *response*—faith (verse 23). If you're not sure you've ever started a relationship with God, talk to him. Tell him something like this: "God, I know I've wronged you. I trust that Jesus died for my sins. Thank you for making me your friend. Help me live close to you." Check out *Trust*, the first book in the DEEPER series, to learn more about what it means to follow Jesus as your Savior and Lord.

- Have a look at **Revelation 7:9-10** for a snapshot of God's crowd at the end of time.

- Don't miss **1 Peter 2:4-10** for more on God's plan for you to connect with him and his people. In case you doubt that building a people is a huge deal to God, look at just a few of the many other spots throughout the Bible where he talks it up: **Genesis 17:7, 12; Exodus 6:7; Leviticus 26:12; Jeremiah 31:33; Ezekiel 11:20, 36:28; 2 Corinthians 6:16; Hebrews 8:10;** and **Revelation 21:3-4.**

3. MEET GOD'S FRIENDS

You need friends who follow Jesus

Hebrews 10:24

And let us consider how we may spur one another on toward love and good deeds.

➔   **START** Trying to do life all by yourself is like crawling into a sewer and pulling the lid shut tight—no light, no warmth, and the situation stinks right from the start! God has a better plan for you. God surrounds you with all kinds of people—from parents and siblings to peers, mentors, and strangers—with whom you can share God's love. And of everyone he puts in your life, there's a spectacular subset you need like none other: You need to hang with people who hang close to God.

Why would you want Christian friends?

➔   **READ** Hebrews 10:24-25

²⁴And let us consider how we may spur one another on toward love and good deeds, ²⁵not giving up meeting together, as some are in the habit of doing, but encouraging one another—and all the more as you see the Day approaching.

➔   **THINK** Back up: Hebrews 10:19-23 (the passage right before these verses) explains the amazing relationship you have with God because of Jesus. Because of his death, you are free to run into God's throne room. In the very next breath, you hear that you need to live close with people who know God. If you read between the lines, it's a colossal challenge: "You've met God? Now meet his friends!"

So what are you and the whole swarm of believers supposed to do for one another?

That word *spur* literally means you are to "irritate" or "exasperate." But the goal isn't to annoy one another; it's to inspire and motivate one another to care intensely for other people and our world.

One crucial thing has to happen for you to stick tight. Some blow it off. What is it?

That phrase in verse 25, "as you see the Day approaching," is all about the return of Jesus to earth, his "second coming." The point is that you can't get ready for Jesus' return all by your lonesome. You need to hang with the herd of Jesus followers.

➜ **LIVE** Who's helped you get closer to God? How?

What scares you off from building Christian friendships? If you've had a tough time making spiritually solid friends, what can you do about it? Whom can you ask for help?

If you could invent a perfect Christian friend, what would she or he look like?

That's nice, but it might not be realistic. After all, it's not fair to expect more of others than you expect of yourself. Read the description you just wrote. Is this the kind of person you strive to be? Why—or why not?

You'll never pursue Christian friendships if you're not convinced you need them. So how much do you think you need friends who follow Jesus? And what about the flip side of that question: How much do other Christians need you?

➜   **WRAP** God's Word doesn't tell you to ditch friends who aren't into God—more on that later. But you can't thrive without at least one or two trustworthy people who prod you to do life with God as your Master. Superficial friendships won't get you what you need. You need to know whom you can count on—and what you can to do to encourage each other along.

»   MORE THOUGHTS TO MULL

▪   Just chillin' is one of the best things you can do with Christian friends—you need that time to socialize. But you also need spiritual stretching. What else can you accomplish by being with others who believe in God?

- So you go to church. How well does your crowd spur you to do what's right—and how do you feel about that? Put a dot on the line below: ·

Total fun and games with no spiritual point	Excessively serious with no chance to breathe

- How do you grow when the Christians around you don't seem to be in the same spot as you? (They want nothing to do with God, for example, or they're gung-ho for God—but in a scary way.)

» MORE SCRIPTURES TO DIG

- Look at what **Ecclesiastes 4:9-10, 12** says about the worth of friends: "Two are better than one, because they have a good return for their labor: If they fall down, they can help each other up. But pity those who fall and have no one to help them up!...Though one may be overpowered, two can defend themselves. A cord of three strands is not quickly broken."

- **Hebrews 3:13** says to "encourage one another," and it adds that you and your believing friends should act to encourage each other "daily." Look it up and see why.

- In **John 17:1-26** Jesus prays for all his followers in all times and all places. His prayer tells you loads about bonding with your Christian brothers and sisters.

- Later in *Stick*, you'll look at **1 Corinthians 12:18-27**, a funny jab at why Christians need one another. Take a peek now. While you're at it, check out **1 Corinthians 13**. It's the Bible's "Love Chapter," a stunningly beautiful yet pointed description of how we can get along. You hear it read at weddings, but its message is meant for all of life.

4. GODCHASERS

What to do with Christian friends

2 Timothy 2:22

Flee the evil desires of youth and pursue righteousness, faith, love and peace,

along with those who call on the Lord out of a pure heart.

➜ **START** You probably didn't wake up this morning and find you'd received a personal message from some major Christian leader—like a text message from the pope or an e-mail from Billy Graham. Yet Timothy wasn't that much older than you when the great apostle Paul sent him a letter that later became the book of 1 Timothy in the Bible. A few years after that, Paul scribbled his "son in the faith" another note. That letter—written just months before Paul was killed for preaching about Jesus—takes Timothy back to the basics, such as what Christian friends are all about.

Maybe you already have a lot of friends who follow Jesus, or maybe you're looking for some fresh ones. Your aim isn't to collect believer-friends like fast-food toys and then toss them in a bin. So once you've got 'em, what are you supposed to do with 'em?

➜ **READ** 2 Timothy 2:22

> [22]Flee the evil desires of youth and pursue righteousness, faith, love and peace, along with those who call on the Lord out of a pure heart.

➜ **THINK** Paul might sound like a wheezing geezer ranting against "those young people today." But what do you think Paul means by "evil desires of youth"?

Later in his letter, Paul fills out what evil looks like, and it's not all sex, drugs, and brain-rotting rock-and-roll. Most sin looks very everydayish: "People will be lovers of themselves, lovers of money, boastful, proud, abusive, disobedient to their parents, ungrateful, unholy, without love, unforgiving, slanderous, without self-control, brutal, not lovers of the good, treacherous, rash, conceited, lovers of pleasure rather than lovers of God—having a form of godliness but denying its power" (2 Timothy 3:2-5).

That's the nasty stuff God wants you to flee. (In fact, the vibe of Paul's original language is stronger—more like "flee and keep fleeing.") But you can't just run away from the bad. There's good stuff to pursue. So what should you "chase and keep on chasing"?

"Righteousness" sounds uptight, but it boils down to acting properly in relationships. "Faith" isn't just about a belief in your head; it's about a trusting commitment from the heart. "Love" is unselfish concern for others, and "peace" is total well-being.

So here's the simple yet significant question: With whom should you chase after all of that? Why is this important?

➜   **LIVE** How do your friends influence how you live?

Pretend you're using an old-school balancing scale in science class. On one side are the friends who pull you closer to God. On the other side sit friends who pull you away. Which side weighs more?

Of all the people in your life, who looks the most like Paul's picture of someone who flees evil and chases good, acting from a pure heart? What are you doing to grow your friendship with that person?

→ **WRAP** If you want to grow close to God, you've got three tasks: 1) Flee evil. 2) Chase God and his goodness. 3) Find people who'll do the first two tasks with you. Every new day is a fresh chance to choose to follow God—but the trip is always better when you take it with friends.

» MORE THOUGHTS TO MULL

- Get personal: Name three evil things you're fleeing, and three good things you're chasing.

- Powerful relationships don't happen only with peers. Can you name some older teenagers or adults who are deeply committed to your spiritual growth?

- Chat with a friend: Make a concrete plan for how you want to get closer to God *together.*

» MORE SCRIPTURES TO DIG

- As close as you and your crowd might be, you didn't invent the idea of friendship. David and Jonathan are probably the best-known pair of friends in the Bible. You can spot them in **1 Samuel 18:1-3**, as well as **1 Samuel 20** where Jonathan risks his life for David. **Proverbs 17:17** dishes up a tight description of a friend. And in **John 15:5** Jesus startles his followers by calling them friends.

- Check **Isaiah 41:8-10** to see what God calls Abraham. Then look at the promises God makes to that amazing Old Testament follower of God—and to you.

- Don't overlook the verses in **2 Timothy 2:20-21**, which lead up to the key verse for this chapter. Paul tells Timothy that every big house has a variety of dishes. As one translation puts it, "The expensive utensils are used for special occasions, and the cheap ones are for everyday use" (2:20 NLT). Paul isn't discussing the good points of china versus paper plates. His point is that people who cleanse themselves from evil are useful to God. Ponder this: "If you keep yourself pure, you will be a special utensil for honorable use. Your life will be clean, and you will be ready for the Master to use you for every good work" (2:21 NLT). There's a reason you want to ditch evil and seek good—it's so God can use you.

- You can be sure the apostle Paul wasn't wasting his dying words just to hear himself speak. His goal was to pour a lifetime of hard-earned wisdom into young Timothy. Read **Proverbs 2:1-15** for some more "back when I was your age" stuff. Write down some of the positive results that come to those who follow God's wise ways.

5. OUT OF THE IGLOO

God wants you to spread his care

Matthew 28:19-20

"Therefore go and make disciples of all nations,

baptizing them in the name of the Father and of the Son and of the Holy Spirit,

and teaching them to obey everything I have commanded you."

➜   **START** Some groups of Christians are like igloos—toasty if you're on the inside, but as chilly as a blizzard if you're not. That's not part of God's plan. Love starts with him. And he intends for his warmth to spread not just to Christians, but also to people who don't yet know him—people all over the world. God wants to crack open the igloo and send you—and every other believer—out to the mobs of humanity who need his love. He's building a people, and he wants that community to keep on growing—forever.

Why would you want to spread God's care—to people nearby or to people you don't even know?

➜   **READ** Matthew 28:18-20

[18]Then Jesus came to them and said, "All authority in heaven and on earth has been given to me. [19]Therefore go and make disciples of all nations, baptizing them in the name of the Father and of the Son and of the Holy Spirit, [20]and teaching them to obey everything I have commanded you. And surely I am with you always, to the very end of the age."

➜   **THINK** Those words come at the very end of the book of Matthew. They're some of Jesus' final words—a command so exceedingly important it's called the Great Commission.

Jesus tells us to go. What are we supposed to make? What are we supposed to do? What are we supposed to teach?

We're told to go to "all nations." Besides dropping out of school and packing yourself in a crate bound for Ukarumpa (it's in Papua New Guinea, in case you're wondering), how can you do that? Any ideas?

Jesus spoke this Bible chunk to all believers—that is, he gave us a *group assignment* to make followers (or "disciples"), teaching people everywhere to trust and obey him totally. Only some of us will travel to places where no one has ever heard of him. But Jesus intends for all of us to join that global effort by praying (Matthew 9:35-38) and giving financial support (2 Corinthians 9:1-14). But don't miss this: Your major role is to start in your own backyard—right now—spreading God's love and care to the people around you (Acts 1:8; 5:42).

➡ **LIVE** How are you doing at spreading God's care and friendship to people you know?

What's the best way to talk to people about God's love?

Trick question. Sharing about God usually starts with actions, showing others the same kindness God shows you (Matthew 7:12). Your message is reinforced by how you act in general (Matthew 5:13-16; 1 Peter 2:12). When you do get a chance to speak up, keep 1 Peter 3:15 in mind: "In your hearts revere Christ as Lord. Always be prepared to give an answer to everyone who asks you to give the reason for the hope that you have. But do this with gentleness and respect." Gentle. Respectful. The same way you want others to talk to you.

Jesus' bold command to spread his love near and far might scare you. But how does it make you feel to know God trusts you with such a crucial assignment?

→   **WRAP** God doesn't give Christians his flaming love to keep our own toes toasty. He aims to build an ever-expanding group of friends who belong to him—friends who honor him as Master and rely on his care now and forever, and whose hearts beat with compassion for all people.

» MORE THOUGHTS TO MULL

- When have you blasted others with an icy chill and left them feeling less than loved?

- Who in your immediate world needs God's warmth the most?

- How can you and some Christian friends work together to help others experience God's care?

» MORE SCRIPTURES TO DIG

- Now that you know about the Great Commission, check out **Acts 1:8**, where Jesus makes a "Great Prediction" spelling out *how* and *where* his people will spread the news about his love: "But you will receive power when the Holy Spirit comes on you; and you will be my witnesses in Jerusalem, and in all Judea and Samaria, and to the ends of the earth." From their hometown of Jerusalem, Jesus' followers will take the news of who he is and what he's done to the far reaches of the planet.

- "All nations" literally means "all peoples." God wants to spread his care not just to political nations but also to people of every language and ethnicity. In **Matthew 5:46-47** and **Luke 10:29-37** Jesus offers more insight into where he wants us to go. Actually, it's more an issue of *who* than where. He wants us to spread his love to everyone around us, including the people we might not like.

- God doesn't want anyone left outside the warmth of his love. See what he says in **2 Peter 3:9**.

- Jesus tops off his command to "Go!" with massively comforting words. Look back at **Matthew 28:20** to catch his point.

6. HANGING TIGHT

Getting non-Christian friends

Mark 2:17

Jesus said to them, "It is not the healthy who need a doctor, but the sick.

I have not come to call the righteous, but sinners."

➡ **START** It's no sweat picking out the classmate who causes major trouble and frustrates the teachers—and it's not very smart to choose to sit in the desk next to such a wild child. Preachers and youth pastors often coach you to run from the wrong crowd so you don't get sucked into sin. And who hasn't heard a parent begin a sentence with, "I don't like you hanging out with..."? But if God wants you to "Go!" and "Love!" and "Make disciples!" you can't exactly hide from people who dabble in evil—or even those who seem to dive into it headfirst. If you want wisdom on how to get along with people who don't follow God, start by taking a look at the life of Jesus.

Should Christians have non-Christian friends? Why—or why not?

➡ **READ** Mark 2:13-17

¹³Once again Jesus went out beside the lake. A large crowd came to him, and he began to teach them. ¹⁴As he walked along, he saw Levi son of Alphaeus sitting at the tax collector's booth. "Follow me," Jesus told him, and Levi got up and followed him.

¹⁵While Jesus was having dinner at Levi's house, many tax collectors and sinners were eating with him and his disciples, for there were many who followed him. ¹⁶When the teachers of the law who were Pharisees saw him eating with the sinners and tax collectors, they asked his disciples: "Why does he eat with tax collectors and sinners?"

¹⁷On hearing this, Jesus said to them, "It is not the healthy who need a doctor, but the sick. I have not come to call the righteous, but sinners."

➜   **THINK** What kind of people follow Jesus? How does he treat them?

You probably know "Levi son of Alphaeus" by another name—Matthew, as in the first guy in the Bible's famous gospel quartet of Matthew, Mark, Luke, and John. Matthew is a tax collector—a hated profession full of bottom-feeders who cheat taxpayers and collaborate with the Roman occupiers.

The religious leaders known as Pharisees are more into keeping rules than living in a real relationship with God. So how would you answer the Pharisees' big quiz for Jesus: Why does he eat with "sinners"? Better yet, explain how Jesus responds to their question.

Is Jesus blind to the problems of the people in this scene? How do you know?

The Pharisees slap the label *sinner* on anyone who refuses to follow their precise set of rules. And they consider eating with a "sinner" to be the same as taking part in their sin. Unlike the Pharisees, Jesus recognizes that all of us have wandered from God's path (Isaiah 53:6) and all of us are sinners (Romans 3:23), including people like the Pharisees! *All of us* need Jesus' spiritual doctoring.

➜ **LIVE** So what do you think Jesus does when he hangs out with people who run amuck of God's rules? What does he not do?

Explain it in your own words: How should you get along with non-Christian friends—and why?

When you hang out with people who aren't big into Jesus, how is pulling them closer to him part of your plan?

➜ **WRAP** Jesus jumps into the gory mess of people's lives, but his aim isn't to join in their sin. Instead, he aims to love and to heal them. So when you hang tight with non-Christian friends, what's *your* goal?

»   MORE THOUGHTS TO MULL

- Jesus calls himself a doctor to the sick. Explain what kind of healing he's trying to provide for all of us.

- When have you been told to avoid a peer? Did you listen? What happened?

- If the Pharisees regard everyone else as spiritual slime, what do you suppose they think about themselves? When have you had their "pharisaical" attitudes?

»   MORE SCRIPTURES TO DIG

- Jesus has another famous meal with a different scandalous tax collector when he summons that wee guy named Zacchaeus down from a tree and then invites himself to dinner at Zach's house. Catch the scoop in **Luke 19:1-9**, and don't miss how Zach's life is radically altered by his encounter with Jesus.

- The dinner scenes with Matthew and Zacchaeus aren't the only times Jesus hangs out with "sinners" who are totally rejected by other religious leaders of their day. Flip to **John 4:1-42** and read his conversation with a Samaritan woman who is outcast not only because of her non-Jewish ancestry, but also for her gender. And look at **John 8:1-11** to see how Jesus rescues a sinful woman who's about to be stoned to death.

- Jesus tells three of his most famous stories in response to the Pharisees muttering, "This man welcomes sinners and eats with them." Check out the parables of the Lost Sheep, the Lost Coin, and the Lost Son in **Luke 15:1-31.**

7. TUGGED INTO TRAFFIC

Too tight with people who don't follow Jesus

2 Corinthians 6:14

Do not be yoked together with unbelievers. For what do righteousness and wickedness have in common?

Or what fellowship can light have with darkness?

➔   **START** Your tiny-tyke years were chock full of street-crossing lessons. Time and again Mom or Dad walked you to the curb, and you watched boggle-eyed as cars and trucks whizzed by—just inches from your nose. For years a parent would clutch your hand as you scampered together across streets and parking lots. When you got a little older, they spied on you as you practiced crossing by yourself. Despite all your proven street smarts, there are still roads you ought not cross—even if you're dared, pushed, or enticed by something on the other side. Not unless you want to be roadsmear under the wheels of a tractor-trailer.

What's the danger in having non-Christian friends? How can those friendships clobber your relationship with God?

➔   **READ** 2 Corinthians 6:14-18

14Do not be yoked together with unbelievers. For what do righteousness and wickedness have in common? Or what fellowship can light have with darkness? 15What harmony is there between Christ and Belial? Or what does a believer have in common with an unbeliever? 16What agreement is there between the temple of God and idols? For we are the temple of the living God. As God has said: "I will live with them and walk among them, and I will be their God, and they will be my people." 17Therefore, "Come out from them and be separate, says the Lord. Touch no unclean thing, and I will receive you." 18And, "I will be a Father to you, and you will be my sons and daughters, says the Lord Almighty."

➔   **THINK** So what exactly are you supposed to avoid doing with "unbelievers"—that is, people who don't follow Jesus? Why is that a bad thing?

A yoke is a hunk of wood that lashes big animals together for plowing and pulling. It forces the animals to go in the same direction. So the gist of "Do not be yoked together" is "Don't team up with those who are unbelievers" (NLT) or "Do not join yourselves to them" (NCV). By the way, "Belial" is another name for Satan that means "scoundrel."

So what should you do when you find yourself "unequally yoked," tied tight with someone who's dragging you into danger?

Your first impulse can't be to cut off every sketchy friend, or you'll miss out on God's purpose of building a people. But sometimes you're smart to put some distance between you and the people who consistently drag you down.

➔   **LIVE** When have you been tight with someone who yanked you in the wrong direction? What happened?

Share what you think this Bible chunk is saying:

Having non-Christian friends	OK	Not OK
Having close non-Christian friends	OK	Not OK
Having a non-Christian best friend	OK	Not OK
Having a non-Christian boyfriend or girlfriend	OK	Not OK
Having a non-Christian spouse	OK	Not OK

The closer and bigger the relationship, the better the chance that it will control you. So where did you draw the line of "Not OK"? Why draw it there?

➜   **WRAP** If you're bound too tightly to a friend who isn't headed toward God, that's trouble—a situation no less hazardous than getting hauled into the mayhem of rush-hour traffic. If you have to wonder whether a friendship is pulling you in the wrong direction, there's a good chance it is. It's only when you're tightly tied both to Jesus and to his followers that you can hope to be a real friend to nonbelievers without getting pulled off somewhere unsafe. And that's no yoke.

» MORE THOUGHTS TO MULL

- How do your best friends pull you closer to Jesus? What do they do that yanks you away from him? If Jesus were literally tugging you one way and your friends were tugging you another, who would win?

- Ask a few mature Christians if they see you wanting friends and fun that drag you in the wrong direction. If they spot a problem, what are you going to do about it?

- So how can you help people who need a relationship with God but also push you to do wrong?

- Look at the passage again. What does God promise if you ditch evil? (Hint: Obeying God doesn't *make* you a Christian, but it lets you *experience* life as his daughter or son. Because of Jesus, you already have God's acceptance; but steering clear of sin is the only way to enjoy closeness to him.)

» MORE SCRIPTURES TO DIG

- Being yoked to nonbelievers is bad. But the Bible tells of another yoke that's exceptionally good. See, if you're a Christian, you're already firmly attached to Jesus. In **Matthew 11:28-30** he says, "Come to me, all you who are weary and burdened, and I will give you rest. Take my yoke upon you and learn from me, for I am gentle and humble in heart, and you will find rest for your souls. For my yoke is easy and my burden is light." When you let Jesus take charge of where you go, you'll always head in the right direction.

- You might picture the people who lived back in Bible times as prisses who could never understand nor cope with the pressures of modern life. But you don't have to read much of the Old Testament to see that back then, people were into evils that went way past PG-13, from child sacrifice to idol worship, incest, and witchcraft. The New Testament knows all about "those who practice magic arts, the sexually immoral, the murderers, the idolaters and everyone who loves and practices falsehood" (**Revelation 22:15**). The writers of Scripture were experts at discerning real danger.

8. STANDING UP TO PEER FEAR

Pleasing God rather than people

Galatians 1:10

Am I now trying to win human approval, or God's approval? Or am I trying to please people?

If I were still trying to please people, I would not be a servant of Christ.

➜ **START** Janessa was dazed when her two best friends told her to quit reading her Bible during study breaks at the library. They said it made *them* look bad—and it made *her* look like a religious freak. Janessa wasn't trying to cause a scene, make a point, or look holier-than-the-rest-of-the-library. She was even using her ultra-slim, ultra-inconspicuous New Testament. She was just reading—and praying without moving her lips. She knew she had every right to open her Bible—and to shut her eyes. What was their problem?

When have you had to stand up to what people thought of you—for being a Christian or for anything else?

➜ **READ** Galatians 1:6-10

⁶I am astonished that you are so quickly deserting the one who called you by the grace of Christ and are turning to a different gospel—⁷which is really no gospel at all. Evidently some people are throwing you into confusion and are trying to pervert the gospel of Christ. ⁸But even if we or an angel from heaven should preach a gospel other than the one we preached to you, let that person be under God's curse! ⁹As we have already said, so now I say again: If anybody is preaching to you a gospel other than what you accepted, let that person be under God's curse!

¹⁰Am I now trying to win human approval, or God's approval? Or am I trying to please people? If I were still trying to please people, I would not be a servant of Christ.

➜   **THINK** In this hugely significant passage, the apostle Paul fights for the core of Christian belief—the truth that God offers salvation to all who trust that Jesus died for their sins. Weirdly, Paul has to resist pressure from people who are supposed to be on his side. Whether you face down someone who wants to force you to give up your faith—or you just want to obey God in something a lot less heroic—Paul coaches you to please God, rather than playing to your peers.

What dumb thing are the people in Galatia doing? What does Paul think of their "different gospel"?

The rest of this Bible book—especially chapter 3—unpacks the wacky beliefs these Galatians were following: They thought they could earn God's love by keeping rules. But the truth is Christians keep God's commands not so God will love us, but because God *already* loves us. The Galatians had totally ditched the message of God's grace, his unearned kindness and care. Not only that, but they were also ditching God himself, the one who invited them—and still invites us—to be his friends for free.

Who is Paul trying to keep happy? Whose opinion does he disregard?

➔ **LIVE** How do your peers sway your attitudes, words, and actions?

When have you put what God wants ahead of what your friends want? Back up your answer with examples.

Does taking God's side make you any less of a friend? Explain.

➔ **WRAP** As King of the universe, Jesus deserves your total obedience. When you trust Jesus, you crown him Lord of your life. But that doesn't mean you love your friends any less. Jesus said you should "let your light shine before others, that they may see your good deeds and glorify your Father in heaven" (Matthew 5:16). Sometimes as a follower of Jesus you'll need to stand against the crowd. But sometimes doing right makes both God and people smile.

» MORE THOUGHTS TO MULL

- How often do you face situations where you can't please both God and people? What's the clash?

- Is it okay for Christians to stand up for something as fiercely as Paul did? Why—or why not?

- Ask a mature Christian to shake you awake if he or she spots you caving to peer fear.

» MORE SCRIPTURES TO DIG

- When push comes to shove, don't ditch God's commands by doing whatever it takes to get people to love you. In **2 Corinthians 8:21** Paul aims to please both God and other believers.

- Back up and read **Galatians 1:1-5**, where Paul explains right from the start the truth he stands for: Jesus is the one who gave himself to rescue us from evil, thus setting us free from the penalty and power of sin.

- In **Acts 5:28-29** some religious leaders threatened to jail Peter and John for preaching about Jesus. But these guys knew whom they had to follow: "We must obey God rather than human beings!"

- Read **Acts 6:8–8:3** for the full story of Stephen, who stood up to opponents of the early church and was the first Christian killed for his faith in Jesus.

- When you're pummeled by your peers—and tempted to go along with whatever they want—give **Luke 12:4-12** a look.

9. CAN'T BUY ME LOVE

Becoming a friend worth having

John 13:14

Now that I, your Lord and Teacher, have washed your feet,

you also should wash one another's feet.

➜ **START** Money can't buy happiness, but it can borrow a few friends. Outside your house you could toss up a swimming pool with multilevel waterslides—and inside, carve out a not-so-mini arcade and an eye-popping, ear-bursting home theater with multiple game systems. With playthings like that, you'd be a real friend magnet. Until someone else throws a better party.

What's the best way to get friends?

➜ **READ** John 13:4-5, 12-14

⁴[Jesus] got up from the meal, took off his outer clothing, and wrapped a towel around his waist. ⁵After that, he poured water into a basin and began to wash his disciples' feet, drying them with the towel that was wrapped around him.

¹²When he had finished washing their feet, he put on his clothes and returned to his place. "Do you understand what I have done for you?" he asked them. ¹³"You call me 'Teacher' and 'Lord,' and rightly so, for that is what I am. ¹⁴Now that I, your Lord and Teacher, have washed your feet, you also should wash one another's feet.

➜ **THINK** You probably don't have the option of handing out cash or prizes to make friends, but maybe you wish you did. Jesus unleashes a more dazzling, durable way to win friends. As the clock ticks down the final hours before his crucifixion, he shows his followers "the full extent of his love" (John 13:1 NIV). Then he commands us to act the same way. If you want to be a friend worth having, Jesus demonstrates how.

Jesus does a crazy thing to show love to his closest friends: He washes their feet. Why do that?

Picture those disciples: burly, sandal-wearing men who spend their days clomping down dusty dirt roads. It's a recipe for filthy, stinking feet. By untying his guys' sandals and scrubbing their feet, Jesus performed a practical, necessary deed. But foot washing was the job for a household's lowliest servant. Unlike Jesus, none of the disciples seized this obvious opportunity to serve. In fact, the book of Luke shows them hotly debating which one of them is the greatest (Luke 22:24).

What does Jesus expect his followers to learn from his act of servanthood?

➡   **LIVE** Suppose you were God. King of the universe. Ruler of all. Tell how you'd expect to be treated.

What do you think of what Jesus did?

People today won't get the point if you just snatch their shoes and socks and powerwash their toes. But Philippians 2:3-4 tells what genuine servanthood looks like in any time and place: "Do nothing out of selfish ambition or vain conceit. Rather, in humility value others above yourselves, not looking to your own interests but each of you to the interests of the others." Servanthood doesn't mean you let others stomp on you. Instead, you make their needs as important as your own.

True or false: Taking the role of a servant can help you make and maintain friends. Explain your answer.

➜   **WRAP** Do you want a collection of friends who care about your needs as much as they care about their own? That's the love God wants to grow among his people, a kind of care that sticks people together forever. If you grow in showing that Jesus-like mindset toward other people, you won't have to buy friends. People will beg to be around you.

»   MORE THOUGHTS TO MULL

- Do something today that honors another person, putting his or her interests before yours.

- Who do you know—someone nearby or someone famous—who knows how to serve like Jesus? How do people respond to that person's attitude and actions?

- What's the difference between being a chump and being a Jesus-like servant?

» MORE SCRIPTURES TO DIG

- The mother of two of Jesus' closest followers once tried to score the best seats in heaven for her boys by kneeling before Jesus and begging that James and John be allowed to sit at the Lord's left and right. The guys weren't embarrassed by their loud-mouthed mom, but the other disciples roared. Jesus called them together and said the real path to greatness is the low path, not the high road. He said, "Whoever wants to become great among you must be your servant" (Matthew 20:26). Catch the whole story in **Matthew 20:20-28**.

- While you're looking at Matthew 20, don't miss a couple more essential truths from that event. In **Matthew 20:25** Jesus points out that it's human nature to rub your rank in other people's faces. But Jesus did just the opposite. In **Matthew 20:28** he outlines his one-of-a-kind approach to life: "The Son of Man did not come to be served, but to serve, and to give his life as a ransom for many."

- Read **Philippians 2:1-11** for a summary of Jesus' intense unselfishness. It's woven together with details on how you can imitate him. You might be surprised to learn this passage makes servanthood sound downright beautiful, and the poetic words of verses 6-11 were probably lyrics sung by early Christians.

- Hundreds of years before Jesus was born, the Old Testament told of a "servant" who would arrive on the scene to take up our pain and bear our sufferings. Check out **Isaiah 53:1-12** for an amazing description of Jesus' ultimate sacrifice—his death on the cross for humankind's sins.

10. GOD'S BIG COMMANDS

God's top rules for getting along

Exodus 20:12-17

Honor your father and your mother...You shall not murder. You shall not commit adultery.

You shall not steal. You shall not give false testimony...You shall not covet.

➜   **START** When God plopped human beings onto earth, he didn't leave us to make up our own rules for doing life. He gave us a top 10 list of gigantic guidelines—four that tell us how to get along with him, and six that say how to get along with our fellow humans. They're basic. They're big. And the Ten Commandments leave no doubt about the attitudes and actions God expects of all people. The whole Bible spells out how to do relationships God's way, but these are the indispensable starters.

Most people aim to live by a few simple principles that outline the right way to treat others. What are yours?

➜   **READ** Exodus 20:1-4, 7-8, 12-17
¹And God spoke all these words:

²"I am the Lord your God, who brought you out of Egypt, out of the land of slavery.

³"You shall have no other gods before me.

⁴"You shall not make for yourself an image in the form of anything in heaven above or on the earth beneath or in the waters below.

⁷"You shall not misuse the name of the Lord your God, for the Lord will not hold anyone guiltless who misuses his name.

⁸"Remember the Sabbath day by keeping it holy.

¹²"Honor your father and your mother, so that you may live long in the land the Lord your God is giving you.

¹³"You shall not murder.

¹⁴"You shall not commit adultery.

¹⁵"You shall not steal.

¹⁶"You shall not give false testimony against your neighbor.

¹⁷"You shall not covet your neighbor's house. You shall not covet your neighbor's wife, or his male or female servant, his ox or donkey, or anything that belongs to your neighbor."

➜   **THINK** God's four first-and-foremost rules forbid giving the top spot in your life to anyone or anything but him. His next six rules relay his main points for getting along with people. Don't miss this detail: To "honor" parents means both to respect and to prize them highly. "Murder" is premeditated killing, including suicide. "Adultery" covers sex outside of marriage. "Stealing" applies to taking stuff that isn't yours—or trying to own people. "False testimony" is lying of any kind. And "coveting" is longing for someone else's stuff—computers, cars, wardrobe, looks, girlfriend/boyfriend...

If you took a poll of your peers, how many would agree that following God's rules is a good idea? On what points would they disagree?

Name some everyday ways you see people ignore these commands.

➔ **LIVE** Which of God's big rules are toughest for you to follow? How come?

How can following those basic commands make you a better friend?

➔ **WRAP** As Maker and Master of the universe, God decides the what, when, and where of how to treat people well. If you want to enjoy your best-ever friendships, don't skip over his basic points for doing relationships right.

» MORE THOUGHTS TO MULL

- If you're having a hard time with someone, make time to sit down with that person. Admit what you've been doing wrong.

- Got a big issue with any of these commands? Talk to God about it.

- How would your life be different if everyone in your world kept these commands? If you chose to obey God on these points, how would it make your world a better place?

» MORE SCRIPTURES TO DIG

- You're probably not planning on killing anyone—this week, anyway. But don't get smug about your goodness. Calling someone an idiot, Jesus says, is as bad as murder (**Matthew 5:22**). And looking at a guy or girl lustfully counts as adultery (**Matthew 5:27-28**). God's rules aren't just about actions. They're also about attitudes.

- The Bible teaches that people instinctively understand these basic principles of right and wrong. But having that data rattling around in the back of your brain isn't the same as doing what God says. See **Romans 1:18-23** for the scoop on how people reject God's facts about right and wrong.

- As humans we're often blind to the wrongs we do toward God and people. **Psalm 139:23-24** contains an amazing prayer you can use to invite God to shine a spotlight on your life, illuminating areas where you fall short of his plans. His aim isn't to make you feel awful, but to help you live tight with him and people.

- God uses the whole Bible to communicate what real love for him and for others looks like, teaching you his always-true wisdom. Like **2 Timothy 3:16-17** says, "All Scripture is God-breathed and is useful for teaching, rebuking, correcting and training in righteousness, so that all God's people may be thoroughly equipped for every good work." God's Word is the referee you need for the game of life.

11. GETTING DOWN AND DIRTY

The qualities of a friend

Ephesians 5:2

Walk in the way of love, just as Christ loved us and gave himself up for us as a fragrant offering and sacrifice to God.

➜   **START** You clap your hands over your mouth the moment the cuss word flies past your lips. You fume. You've done it again! #@&%*! And there, you did it again! You press your hands over your mouth even harder, letting go only when you stand at the bathroom sink. You've heard your grandpa tell how his mother washed his mouth out with soap whenever he said a bad word. Sure, great-grandma used bar soap, but a squirt of liquid soap on your toothbrush should have the same effect...

God wants you to have incredible qualities of a friend—obeying him with every part of your mouth, mind, and body. How do you think that happens?

➜   **READ** Ephesians 4:25–5:2

²⁵Therefore each of you must put off falsehood and speak truthfully to your neighbor, for we are all members of one body. ²⁶"In your anger do not sin": Do not let the sun go down while you are still angry, ²⁷and do not give the devil a foothold. ²⁸Those who have been stealing must steal no longer, but must work, doing something useful with their own hands, that they may have something to share with those in need.

²⁹Do not let any unwholesome talk come out of your mouths, but only what is helpful for building others up according to their needs, that it may benefit those who listen. ³⁰And do not grieve the Holy Spirit of God, with whom you were sealed for the day of redemption. ³¹Get rid of all bitterness, rage and anger, brawling and slander, along with every form of malice. ³²Be kind and compassionate to one another, forgiving each other, just as in Christ God forgave you.

¹Follow God's example, therefore, as dearly loved children ²and walk in the way of love, just as Christ loved us and gave himself up for us as a fragrant offering and sacrifice to God.

➜ **THINK** This Bible passage rattles off loads of evil things to ditch—and good things to do. They all add up to "the way of love" (5:2). Jot down a half dozen commands that seem major.

When you walk in this "way of love," whose example are you following? How is that possible?

Another version makes that command in Ephesians 5:1 really pop: "Be imitators of God" (NIV)! That's a staggering impossibility—unless you remember 1 John 4:19 from Study 1 of this book: "We love because he first loved us." Here, the apostle Paul is saying much the same thing. You get power to love others when you bask in the fact that Jesus loves you and died for you.

➜ **LIVE** How would you act if you were doing an imitation of God?

In this passage God gets into the down-and-dirty details of what love looks like. Is he just being picky—or do all these points have something to do with being an awesome friend? Explain your answer.

You probably already do great at following some of those commands. Others might poke your conscience. Of all those do's and don'ts, where do you most want to change?

➜   **WRAP** The nitty-gritty qualities of being a friend worth having aren't just about being nice. They aren't a disguise you can plaster on like makeup, or a charming personality that you can turn on or off depending on who's looking. You get these qualities only when you let God radically remake your life. Looking at the list of what God's "way of love" looks like, you might feel you're nowhere near the path God has planned for you. But the longer and tighter you stick with God, the more you start to look like him.

》   **MORE THOUGHTS TO MULL**

▪   Suppose someone wants to snap a picture of your life. What's your "best side"? Where do you do best in being God's kind of friend?

▪   When it comes to imitating God—living a life of love and being a fantastic friend—what's your biggest struggle?

▪   Say it in your own words: How does God help you change?

» MORE SCRIPTURES TO DIG

- Right before this Bible passage, the apostle Paul reminds his readers not to live like people who still pursue evil. Those folks, Paul says, "are hopelessly confused. Their minds are full of darkness; they wander far from the life God gives because they have closed their minds and hardened their hearts against him. They have no sense of shame..." (**Ephesians 4:17-19**, NLT). Your job as a Christian is to ditch those dark ways and become a friend who shocks people with the genuine goodness of your attitudes and actions.

- God wants to make you look like him in massive ways. The list of qualities he's building in you continues in **Ephesians 5:3-20**. Some highlights: Stay sexually pure. Don't wish for stuff that belongs to someone else. Ditch dirty words. Skip getting drunk.

- Here's a mind-boggling concept: The more you see of God, the more you become like him. It says so in **2 Corinthians 3:18**: "And we all, who with unveiled faces contemplate the Lord's glory, are being transformed into his image with ever-increasing glory, which comes from the Lord, who is the Spirit."

- Check out **Philippians 1:6**, where God promises to complete the huge job he's begun in you. God won't quit until you look like him.

12. EXTREME FRIENDSHIP

Love is meant for everyone

Matthew 5:44

"Love your enemies and pray for those who persecute you."

➜   **START** Ever since third grade you've been feuding with the
sorry excuse for a human being who's just plunked down in the desk
in front of you. Last week your squabble erupted afresh when the guy
pelted your house with three dozen eggs—resulting in two giant swaths
of dimpled siding, three shattered windows, and one traumatized family
dog. If that wasn't bad enough, the police interrogated *you*. Your parents
blamed *you*. The only plus about sitting behind him now is that he can't
see your laser-like eyes smoking holes in his skull.

How do you treat people who inflict pain on you?

➜   **READ** Matthew 5:43-48

Jesus said: ⁴³"You have heard that it was said, 'Love your neighbor and hate your enemy.' ⁴⁴But I tell you, love your enemies and
pray for those who persecute you, ⁴⁵that you may be children of
your Father in heaven. He causes his sun to rise on the evil and
the good, and sends rain on the righteous and the unrighteous.
⁴⁶If you love those who love you, what reward will you get? Are
not even the tax collectors doing that? ⁴⁷And if you greet only
your own people, what are you doing more than others? Do not
even pagans do that? ⁴⁸Be perfect, therefore, as your heavenly
Father is perfect."

➜   **THINK** Perfect? Like God? If this command sounds over the
top, breathe deeply. Then answer this: Why does Jesus tell you to "love
your enemies and pray for those who persecute you"? (Look for what
follows "that you may be...")

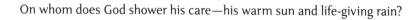

On whom does God shower his care—his warm sun and life-giving rain?

Even pagans who don't know God care about people who love them. How can you do better than that?

➜   **LIVE** If you love people who cause you pain, are you excusing the wrongs they do? Explain.

You've learned that God wants his care to spread around the world and to every person on the planet. No doubt there are some people you'd rather skip. Yet when you love the unlovable and care for the incurable, you're like God. Perfect. Holy. Mature. God never brushes off evil. In fact, he's the only being in the universe who knows how it feels to have the whole human race stand against him (Romans 5:10). But his undeserved kindness busts through our sinfulness and makes us his friends (Colossians 1:21-22). He wants us to pass on to others the love he's given to us.

When you scan your world, who looks easy to love? Why?

Who is more challenging to love? Make a list. Next to each name, jot down one tiny way you can show this person the same brand of kindness God shows us.

➡   **WRAP** You might figure that Jesus received a lot of playground thrashings as a kid. After all, he tells you not just to love your enemies but to "turn your other cheek" (Matthew 5:39 NIRV). One thing shows us for sure that Jesus was no wimp: He was radically tough in his willingness to suffer for our sake. Loving an enemy doesn't mean you're pathetically weak. It proves you're incredibly strong.

❯❯   MORE THOUGHTS TO MULL

- What people in your world act with Christlike kindness? Ask them how they pull it off.

- Think about some of your ugliest thoughts about people. Then ask yourself how you'd feel if God or other people felt that way about you.

- Some of the people who hurt you in life will be fellow Christians. How does the fact that you and your archenemy may one day share a pew in heaven alter how you act now?

❯❯   MORE SCRIPTURES TO DIG

- Your natural instincts tell you to dish back whatever others dish at you. Jesus sums up that mentality in **Matthew 5:38-42**. Then he tells us to go out of our way to be kind to people who cause us pain. Clearly that's a massive challenge, but it's doing love the way Jesus does it.

- You might feel as though you're letting evil slide if you don't take revenge for the wrongs done to you. Actually, when you choose not to repay evil with evil, you stomp on evil by doing good things. "If your enemy is hungry, feed him; if he is thirsty, give him something to drink. In doing this, you will heap burning coals on his head." Look for all of these deep thoughts in **Romans 12:17-21**.

- None of this means you can't ask God to rescue you from people who aim to crush you. Look at **Psalm 25** for some wise words. King David prays for safety. He asks for his enemies' downfall. But David also asks God to forgive his sins, and he invites God to guide him along the right paths in every part of his life.

- You have one enemy who's more evil than any other. And he's one guy you don't have to love. Read about him in **1 Peter 5:8-11**.

13. WORK IT OUT

Four steps for solving conflict

Matthew 18:15

"If a brother or sister sins, go and point out the fault, just between the two of you."

➔   **START** Lots of people figure Christianity is a religion for people who like to get rolled over. Actually, everything Jesus teaches implies you should fight for what's right. He even outlines what to do when someone wrongs you. Sure, some hurts you can overlook. But when you can't let an offense slide—it's too big, it bothers you too much, or it harms someone you're obligated to protect—try these insights from Jesus. You can think of his compact wisdom as *God's Four Steps to Getting Along.*

Suppose you'd like to halt someone's nasty actions. What's your usual plan?

➔   **READ** Matthew 18:15-17

> Jesus said: [15]"If a brother or sister sins, go and point out the fault, just between the two of you. If they listen to you, you have won them over. [16]But if they will not listen, take one or two others along, so that 'every matter may be established by the testimony of two or three witnesses.' [17]If they still refuse to listen, tell it to the church; and if they refuse to listen even to the church, treat them as you would a pagan or a tax collector."

➔   **THINK** The first step is to talk. In private. Screaming doesn't count. Your aim isn't proving you're right but repairing the relationship. So what's the potential payoff of that first step?

You try that. Nothing happens. What's the next step when an opponent continues to act obnoxiously?

The point of taking "one or two others along" is not to gang up on a wrongdoer but to get at the facts. That's what it means for "every matter" to be "established by the testimony of two or three witnesses" (Deuteronomy 19:15).

Getting help doesn't solve the problem. What now?

Once you've tried to solve a problem yourself—and tried again with another observer—your next step is to appeal to an authority. And if you don't immediately get the help you need, that higher-up almost always has a higher higher-up. But things are getting serious now. Think hard: Is the problem big enough to be worth dragging an adult into the situation? What might it cost you?

What's your final step when nothing else works?

Those serious words mean "Have nothing to do with this person!" Sometimes you need to take a break from the friendship—or get out of a situation totally. Take a time-out.

➜   **LIVE** Look at those four steps in everyday language. *Step 1:* Talk in private. *Step 2:* Bring a witness. *Step 3:* Appeal to an authority. *Step 4:* Take a break from the relationship. When have you used steps like these to fix things with a friend? How did it help—or not?

What situations in your life need solving? What's your plan for putting this process to work?

➜   **WRAP** Check this ancient wisdom: "You must not hate your fellow citizen in your heart. If your neighbor does something wrong, tell him about it, or you will be partly to blame. Forget about the wrong things people do to you, and do not try to get even. Love your neighbor as you love yourself. I am the Lord" (Leviticus 19:17-18, NCV).

» MORE THOUGHTS TO MULL

- As tough as this process sounds, other options are worse—in fact, you probably have a few ugly labels for people who rocket past these steps. Like, what do you call a person who badmouths you to others instead of bringing an issue directly to you? Or a peer who always runs straight to a parent or a teacher? Or someone who feels offended and instantly breaks off a friendship?

- How do you expect people will react if you try to live by these principles?

- If you're stuck in a particularly tangled situation, ask a mature Christian to help you make a plan to sort things out.

- One caution: There are times when it's not wise to go straight to someone who's hurt you. It's not your job to confront, for example, someone who has abused you physically or sexually—or anyone else who makes you feel unsafe. If you or someone you know is facing that kind of situation, take the problem to a trusted adult who can get you or your friend the right help.

» MORE SCRIPTURES TO DIG

- **Proverbs 19:11** sums up the right approach to small offenses: "A person's wisdom yields patience; it is to one's glory to overlook an offense."

- Don't miss **1 Peter 4:8**, which says, "Love covers over a multitude of sins." That doesn't mean, "Sweep sins under the rug." It means love doesn't focus on every little fault.

- Whenever you talk with an opponent, speak the way you want to be spoken to. Look at **Ephesians 4:15** for a tight summary of the right way to talk.

- **Romans 12:18** says, "If it is possible, as far as it depends on you, live at peace with everyone." The Bible isn't stupid. You won't win over everyone. But it never hurts to try.

14. WILDLY GIFTED

You have abilities to offer your world

1 Corinthians 12:7

Now to each one the manifestation of the Spirit is given for the common good.

➜ **START** Whenever her church youth group got together, Hailey stuck to the back wall. She didn't sing. She never spoke up in Bible study. And she'd sooner die than do skits. The last time the group played ultimate Frisbee, she got popped in the nose and gushed blood all over her top. So when a friend's mom invited her to help teach Sunday school to three-year-olds, she hesitated. Yet after a few weeks with the tots, she knew she'd found her niche. She had a voice. Things to say. She had a gift.

How would you react if someone said you're "gifted"?

➜ **READ** 1 Corinthians 12:4-11

4There are different kinds of gifts, but the same Spirit distributes them. 5There are different kinds of service, but the same Lord. 6There are different kinds of working, but in all of them and in everyone it is the same God at work.

7Now to each one the manifestation of the Spirit is given for the common good. 8To one there is given through the Spirit a message of wisdom, to another a message of knowledge by means of the same Spirit, 9to another faith by the same Spirit, to another gifts of healing by that one Spirit, 10to another miraculous powers, to another prophecy, to another distinguishing between spirits, to another speaking in different kinds of tongues, and to still another the interpretation of tongues. 11All these are the work of one and the same Spirit, and he distributes them to each one, just as he determines.

➜   **THINK** "Spiritual gifts" is a name you might have heard for these unique abilities. Big question: Who gives gifts? Who gets them?

You've got God-given abilities. That news might shock you, since the gifts listed above range from teaching to doing miracles to speaking in new languages. Actually, there are many ways you might react to hearing that God has given you certain gifts. You might be *confident*—you know about these gifts. You might be *confused*—absolutely clueless. Or you might be *curious*—thinking those gifts sound cool. But however you feel, the fact remains: You're gifted.

What are you supposed to do with your gift? Who benefits?

A few of the "spiritual gifts" talked about in this Bible chunk cause gigantic controversy. But the point of the passage is that God has given each Christian special gifts to help build his people. Some gifts look everyday-ish. Others are spectacular, mind-blowing even. But the whole package of what God has put inside you is what you have to offer the world.

➜   **LIVE** What gifts has God given to you—not just spiritual gifts, but all sorts? What are you good at?

How have you seen God use you to help someone? How could that act have involved a spiritual gift?

When have you been jealous and wished you had someone else's assortment of talents?

How can you use your unique qualities to build up your friends—and draw them closer to God?

➜ **WRAP** God doesn't give dumb gifts. Next to introducing friends to Jesus, the biggest gift you can give to your world is *you*. As the poet e.e. cummings wrote, the hardest battle in life is "to be nobody-but-yourself—in a world which is doing its best, night and day, to make you everybody else." Invite God to show you your gifts—and to use you in ways beyond your wildest dreams.

» MORE THOUGHTS TO MULL

- What people or events in life have made you feel totally *ungifted*?

- You don't have to be sure about what gifts God has given to you before you can start being useful to God. What new people-building activity would you like to try?

- If you really want to figure out your own spiritual gifts, talk to your pastor. Or pick up the book *Find Your Fit* (Bethany House, 1998), the youth version of *LifeKeys* for adults. I co-wrote *Find Your Fit* with human resources whiz Jane Kise. It shows how your talents, spiritual gifts, and personality all add up to who you are. You'll never look down on yourself again.

» MORE SCRIPTURES TO DIG

- In **1 Corinthians 12:8-11**, Paul catalogs some of the gifts God gives to believers. There are also other lists and places in the Bible where gifts are discussed in depth, like **1 Corinthians 14:1-30**; **Ephesians 4:11-13**; and **Romans 12:4-8**. The point in each listing? Each ability is uniquely valuable and absolutely necessary.

- Spiritual gifts are only one part of the package of God's gifts to you. Look at the apostle Paul, for example. He has the spiritual gift of apostleship (**Romans 1:1**), which includes the twin abilities to lead multiple churches and to declare the good news across cultures. He also has a talent for tentmaking that determined where he'd preach (**Acts 18:1-4**). He's unafraid of conflict (**Galatians 2:1-15**). And he has a passion to preach where no one else has preached before (**2 Corinthians 10:16**). You, too, have a great mix of gifts inside of you.

- **Galatians 6:4** says to keep your eyes on your own actions and take pride in your God-given strengths, but not to waste your energy comparing yourself to others.

15. THE UNIQUELY NEEDED YOU

You're part of Christ's body

1 Corinthians 12:18

But in fact God has placed the parts in the body, every one of them, just as he wanted them to be.

➜   **START** The fate of the world doesn't hinge on your ability to wiggle your ears. Or the way you can do grotesque moves with a double-jointed shoulder. Or how you can pick your nose with your tongue. But you possess other unique traits that really do matter. Those points don't happen by accident because God himself designed you as an exquisite bundle of gifts, characteristics, and experiences. You're the total package. And get this: When you can bust loose and be yourself, you make this planet a better place.

What weird and wonderful things make you different from most other people?

➜   **READ** 1 Corinthians 12:15-23

[15]Now if the foot should say, "Because I am not a hand, I do not belong to the body," it would not for that reason cease to be part of the body. [16]And if the ear should say, "Because I am not an eye, I do not belong to the body," it would not for that reason cease to be part of the body. [17]If the whole body were an eye, where would the sense of hearing be? If the whole body were an ear, where would the sense of smell be? [18]But in fact God has placed the parts in the body, every one of them, just as he wanted them to be. [19]If they were all one part, where would the body be? [20]As it is, there are many parts, but one body.

[21]The eye cannot say to the hand, "I don't need you!" And the head cannot say to the feet, "I don't need you!" [22]On the contrary, those parts of the body that seem to be weaker are indispensable, [23]and the parts that we think are less honorable we treat with special honor.

➜ **THINK** These talking feet and ears aren't clipped from a zany biology textbook. The apostle Paul is saying individual Christians are like various body parts. Put together, we are the "body of Christ" (1 Corinthians 12:27) with Jesus as the head. Chew on that metaphor, then answer this: Why did God make people so different?

An ear can't exist without the body. An eye can't lop off a hand. So what bad stuff happens when someone gets put down or excluded—at school, church, wherever?

How should we relate to people who seem unimportant?

The parts of the body that seem weak or weird are just as necessary as the parts you show off. Paul delicately points out that hidden body parts—your organs and your innards—are worthy of special respect. The people you might think it's okay to ignore still fulfill a need in your life that no one else can.

➔   **LIVE** When do you battle being yourself? In what situations might you get mocked for displaying the "true you"?

What facts or feelings about yourself do you hide?

If you could share one hidden thing about yourself with one person you trust, what would it be?

➔   **WRAP** No eyeball flings itself from its socket. No toe defects from the foot. These are the facts of life—facts so indisputable, they're laughable. Just as parts of the body need one another, people—especially in the church—need one another. You and the people around you are each absolutely indispensable and irreversibly connected. Be yourself. We can't thrive without you.

» MORE THOUGHTS TO MULL

- When have you rejected someone for being different from you?

- How can you reach out to someone whom you've been keeping at a distance?

- How will you react the next time someone rejects you?

» MORE SCRIPTURES TO DIG

- You can't force people to value you highly. You can, however, control how you treat others. And you can always decide to be confident in yourself, knowing God made you unique. **Psalm 139:13-16** says you are "fearfully and wonderfully made." That word *fearfully* might sound like the way you look when you wake up with whacked-out hair and furry teeth. But *fearfully* actually means "awesomely" or "awe-strikingly." That whole psalm offers massive encouragement that you are God's handiwork. He knew exactly what he was doing when you were being assembled in your mother's womb. He even saw your whole life ahead of time.

- Dive into **Ephesians 4:7-16**. It says that when we don't get along as a body, we're like infants bobbing on an ocean. *Scary.*

- Read the whole passage from which our focus verses are taken—**1 Corinthians 12:12-31**. Look for what happens when one body part is hurting—and how we can respond when one part succeeds.

- We are all part of the body of Christ. Each one of us has an important role to play. But none of us can claim to be the brain in this body. Jesus has that part covered. Check out **Ephesians 4:15**.

16. MAJOR PAINS

Helping friends who are hurting

2 Corinthians 1:3-4

Praise be to the God and Father of our Lord Jesus Christ, the Father of compassion and the God of all comfort,

who comforts us in all our troubles, so that we can comfort those in any trouble

with the comfort we ourselves receive from God.

➜ **START** When Tara's dad fell sick with cancer, slid into a coma, and died, Jamal was the only person who could get through to her. She listened quietly to what Jamal said, thinking about every word. After all, Jamal knew how Tara felt; his own dad had died from a heart attack a couple years before. Tara and Jamal spent long hours talking about how bad the whole thing hurt, how life would change, and how they could survive. To be honest, Tara would have crumpled into a lump of permanent sadness if Jamal hadn't been around.

When has a friend helped you through something painful—major or minor? What did she or he do to help?

➜ **READ** 2 Corinthians 1:3-7

³Praise be to the God and Father of our Lord Jesus Christ, the Father of compassion and the God of all comfort, ⁴who comforts us in all our troubles, so that we can comfort those in any trouble with the comfort we ourselves receive from God. ⁵For just as we share abundantly in the sufferings of Christ, so also our comfort abounds through Christ. ⁶If we are distressed, it is for your comfort and salvation; if we are comforted, it is for your comfort, which produces in you patient endurance of the same sufferings we suffer. ⁷And our hope for you is firm, because we know that just as you share in our sufferings, so also you share in our comfort.

➜ **THINK** Loads of people picture God as a life-wrecking meanie, the source of everything cruel. Here you see God as he really is, "the Father of compassion and the God of all comfort." So what does God do for you when life gets miserable?

What good can come out of your pain?

A ghastly situation won't suddenly feel pleasant just because you know you'll be able to pass along all that you've learned to other hurting people. But it's a fact that someday you'll probably get a chance to turn your hurts into help for others. The apostle Paul boldly declares that whatever happens to him—good or bad—will benefit others. Whatever suffering comes our way, God has an even bigger heap of comfort.

➜ **LIVE** What difficult things have you faced in life—big, small, and every size in-between?

How have you experienced God's comfort in those situations—straight from God and through other people?

If you've received some sort of comfort in difficult times, what help can you offer other hurting people who are in the same or similar circumstances? Who needs what you know?

Name five concrete things you can do to support a hurting friend. Circle the one you find easiest to do.

Comfort isn't just patting people on the back until they feel better. It means getting into their hurt and giving them what they need most—help, consolation, encouragement. Often you can provide comfort by just listening.

➜   **WRAP** Hardly anyone who's going through a tough situation likes to hear that God will use their pain for someone else's gain. But once you can look back and see how God stuck with you through it all, then you might be ready to give others the comfort he gave to you. Turning hurts into help is what friends do.

» MORE THOUGHTS TO MULL

▪ How do you rely on God for help when your life gets hard? What steps do you take to count on him?

▪ When people are suffering, sometimes they may find it hard to hear about how God cares for them. Rather than banging people on the head with the raw facts of God's care, we can show God's love through our own actions. Who in your world is suffering major pain right now? Meet with a couple friends and put your heads together to come up with a practical plan to show that person God's care.

▪ Your age doesn't have to limit what you can do to help people in pain. What big hurts in your school or hometown would you like to address?

- You might be in too much pain to think about doing good things for other people. Do you need some extra support in dealing with certain hurts in your life right now? Where can you get help?

» MORE SCRIPTURES TO DIG

- Paul's life wasn't exactly happy when he wrote this passage. He isn't talking about trivial pains—in fact, he thought he was going to die. Catch the details in **2 Corinthians 1:8-11**. The "province of Asia" Paul mentions is in modern-day Turkey, a few hundred miles from his readers in the Greek city of Corinth. In **2 Corinthians 11:23-29** you can read about other hurts Paul suffered—everything from shipwrecks to stonings.

- **1 Peter 1:3-9** and **James 1:2-5** offer hope when your world gets flipped upside down. **Psalm 145** is a tight message about God's care. And **Romans 8:18** informs you that God's work in you is way bigger than any momentary pain.

- **Romans 8:28-29** tells you that no matter what happens to you, God is working for your good. Some people think that means everything nasty in life is really nice. That's not the point. The real message is that God cares. He's close, even when it doesn't feel like he is. And he's working to make you like Jesus, even when times are tough.

17. OVER THE EDGE

Helping friends who fail

Galatians 6:2

Carry each other's burdens, and in this way you will fulfill the law of Christ.

➜   **START** You aren't surprised when your insanely adventurous friend Kala stands with her toes over the lip of a rocky outcrop more than a couple thousand feet up a mountain trail. But you stop breathing when she loses her balance and slips over the edge. As Kala dangles from a tree root like a pitiful character in a cheesy cable movie, you have just an instant to figure out what to do...

How do you react when you see a friend in trouble?

➜   **READ** Galatians 6:1-5

¹Brothers and sisters, if someone is caught in a sin, you who live by the Spirit should restore that person gently. But watch yourselves, or you also may be tempted. ²Carry each other's burdens, and in this way you will fulfill the law of Christ. ³If any of you think you are something when you are nothing, you deceive yourselves. ⁴Each of you should test your own actions. Then you can take pride in yourself, without comparing yourself to somebody else, ⁵for each of you should carry your own load.

➜   **THINK** Suppose you spot a friend slipping into sin—or *flying* into it while doing a triple backflip. Your job is to "restore" that person, a word that describes the process of carefully setting a broken bone. So what does gently restoring others look like in real life?

What qualifies you to rescue friends who make less-than-the-best choices? What is the danger for you in doing this?

You might think you're too intelligent to heed the apostle Paul's warning, but you really do risk getting sucked into sin unless you live tight with God. In the previous chapter, note how Paul explains what it means to "live by the Spirit." Verse 2 says, "carry each other's burdens," and verse 5 says, "each of you should carry your own load." How can you do both?

When Paul says to help lift "burdens," he picks a word meaning "heavy loads," as in rocks too gigantic for one person to hoist. Teamwork is the only way you can move those boulders. When he says to carry your own "load," he's talking about a soldier's daypack. Everyone on earth has basic personal responsibilities they must shoulder.

➔   **LIVE** Name some ways you take responsibility for yourself—tasks where you don't expect your family, friends, or teachers to lug the weight for you. Name some other areas where you can't get by without others to help you along.

I carry my own load...   I need others to help lift...

When have you tried to talk a friend out of doing something stupid or sinful? What worked—or didn't?

Suppose a friend has flipped over a dangerous edge. How would you involve other people in the rescue?

➜   **WRAP** Nobody else on the planet stands in the exact spot you do and within an arm's length of a unique set of friends, acquaintances, and strangers who need your help. Some feel crushed—you can help lift their burden. Others stumble—but you can help them back to their feet. A few go over the edge—and you might be the only one around to call for more help. And when you're the one needing a lift, you can count on that same crowd to lend you a hand.

» MORE THOUGHTS TO MULL

▪   What's good about taking responsibility for yourself?

▪   When do you find it the most difficult to ask for help?

▪   How can you decide if a friend *really* needs help—or if he's slacking and just wants to dump his load on you?

▪   When a friend's problem gets too big to handle, where do you run for help?

» MORE SCRIPTURES TO DIG

- "So, if you think you are standing firm, be careful that you don't fall!" That's **1 Corinthians 10:12**, wise advice from a section that describes how God's Old Testament people catapulted into sin. We can learn from their bad example. Whenever you assume you're too strong to be tempted, take all of **1 Corinthians 10:1-13** to heart.

- Check **Galatians 5:13-26** to see what makes you a strong helper for others. Some highlights: You steer clear of sin, you're humble, you love others as much as you love yourself, you don't bite, and you let the Holy Spirit control your actions. That's a stunning list. And it's all stuff God does inside of you as you "live by the Spirit" (**Galatians 6:2**).

- Paul says you should celebrate your accomplishments without rubbing your greatness in other people's faces (**Galatians 6:4**). And if you're going to brag, there's really only one thing to talk big about. Like **Jeremiah 9:23-24** says, "Let not the wise boast of their wisdom or the strong boast of their strength or the rich boast of their riches, but let those who boast boast about this: that they understand and know me, that I am the Lord."

18. DUMPED

Friends who let you down

Mark 14:72

Then Peter remembered the word Jesus had spoken to him:

"Before the rooster crows twice you will disown me three times."
And he broke down and wept.

➡ **START** Friends don't let friends do life alone. Then again, sometimes you and a pal go so far in opposite directions that your one-time friend looks like a tiny stick figure in your rearview mirror. Other times a friend exits by taking a flying leap into evil. Or a friend moves away and distance yanks you apart. And—tough to chew on—someday you'll face a buddy's death. Whenever you lose a friend, part of you withers.

When has a friend totally left you down and out?

➡ **READ** Mark 14:66-72

⁶⁶While Peter was below in the courtyard, one of the servant girls of the high priest came by. ⁶⁷When she saw Peter warming himself, she looked closely at him.

"You also were with that Nazarene, Jesus," she said.

⁶⁸But he denied it. "I don't know or understand what you're talking about," he said, and went out into the entryway.

⁶⁹When the servant girl saw him there, she said again to those standing around, "This fellow is one of them." ⁷⁰Again he denied it.

After a little while, those standing near said to Peter, "Surely you are one of them, for you are a Galilean."

⁷¹He began to call down curses, and he swore to them, "I don't know this man you're talking about."

⁷²Immediately the rooster crowed the second time. Then Peter remembered the word Jesus had spoken to him: "Before the rooster crows twice you will disown me three times." And he broke down and wept.

➜ **THINK** Yep—that's Peter, the friend who swore he'd gladly die with Jesus (Mark 14:31). As Jesus is arrested and dragged toward the cross, his disciple follows at a distance, right into the courtyard where Jesus' trial would take place. While Jesus is mocked, beaten, and spit on, Peter is warming his backside by the guards' fire (Mark 14:63-65). And as he lurks in the shadows, Peter renounces his Lord three times, just as Jesus predicted he would do (Mark 14:30).

Who all questions Peter? What exactly does he say each time he disowns Jesus?

Nothing against servant girls, but this brawny guy is getting bullied by a solo ankle-biter. Then she riles up a crowd to accuse Peter. The third time Peter completely denies knowing Jesus, calling down God's wrath if he's lying—a big-time "cross my heart and hope to die, stick a needle in my eye"!

Luke 22:61 reports that the moment the rooster crows, Jesus stares straight at Peter. How does Peter react when he hears the cock-a-doodle-doo? What does he suddenly remember? What does he do?

➜ **LIVE** Pretend you're Peter. How are you feeling right now?

See this situation from the other side: You're *Jesus*. Share what's running through your head.

Imagine a friend somehow leaves you hanging. How does it help you to know Jesus faced the same sad situation?

→ **WRAP** When friends dump you, Jesus understands. When you fail a friend, he understands. Even when you fall down in your friendship with him, he understands. He gets it because he's been there.

» MORE THOUGHTS TO MULL

- When do you feel yanked around by your friends?

- Whom have you disappointed lately? Go straighten it out.

- Think of the most dependable friend you know—for example, an adult who never lets anyone down. Ask her why she's such a stead-fast and loyal friend.

» MORE SCRIPTURES TO DIG

- This is one ugly friend-dumps-friend story. But ponder this: Jesus had already read the script. Even though he knows Peter will deny him one day, Jesus still honors Peter with a spot in his tightest inner circle. You can see the disciples Peter, James, and John in **Mark 5:37-43**, where they watch their Master raise a little girl from the dead. Check **Matthew 17:1-9**, where this same trio sees Jesus glow with heavenly brightness. And in **Mark 13:32-43**, Jesus invites them to keep him company in a shadowy garden as he prays in agony before he heads to the cross.

- Early on, Peter was known for his hot-and-cold trust in Jesus. See him make a splash as he tries to walk on water in **Matthew 14:25-33**. Watch him shave off a guy's ear in **John 18:10-11**. Yet look how he recognizes Jesus as the Son of God in **Matthew 16:13-19**.

- After Jesus rose from the dead, he invited Peter back into tight friendship. Read **John 21:15-19**, where the Lord tells Peter he still loves him—and vice versa.

- Just weeks after Peter ditches Jesus, the Holy Spirit radically transforms Peter into a fearless preacher. Don't miss **Acts 2:22-39** and **Acts 4:12** where Peter shouts for all to hear that his best friend Jesus is the one way to know God. Tradition says Peter was killed for his faith in AD 60.

19. 7000 FRIENDS

Conquering loneliness

1 Kings 19:10

Elijah replied, "I have been very zealous for the Lord God Almighty...I am the only one left."

➔   **START** Without a bit of a recap from past episodes, you might miss the gist of this peak Bible drama. *Main character:* Elijah—a prophet, one of God's major spokespersons of all time. *Last episode:* Elijah stands on a sacred mountaintop, one man against 450 prophets of the fake god Baal. At Elijah's request, God sends fire from heaven to torch a sacrifice—stone altar and all (1 Kings 18:19-40). Baal lost. God won. *Tonight's show:* Elijah totals up his friends, gets zilch, and concludes he's the one-and-only true believer in God. He tells God he'd be happier dead. Hunted by the armies of an evil queen, he hikes for 40 days and crawls into a cave.

How do you keep going when life—especially wanting to do the right thing—leaves you feeling alone?

➔   **READ** 1 Kings 19:9-14

⁹And the word of the Lord came to him: "What are you doing here, Elijah?"

¹⁰He replied, "I have been very zealous for the Lord God Almighty. The Israelites have rejected your covenant, torn down your altars, and put your prophets to death with the sword. I am the only one left, and now they are trying to kill me too."

¹¹The Lord said, "Go out and stand on the mountain in the presence of the Lord, for the Lord is about to pass by."

Then a great and powerful wind tore the mountains apart and shattered the rocks before the Lord, but the Lord was not in the wind. After the wind there was an earthquake, but the Lord was not in the earthquake. ¹²After the earthquake came a fire, but the Lord was not in the fire. And after the fire came a gentle whisper. ¹³When Elijah heard it, he pulled his cloak over his face and went out and stood at the mouth of the cave.

Then a voice said to him, "What are you doing here, Elijah?"

¹⁴He replied, "I have been very zealous for the Lord God Almighty. The Israelites have rejected your covenant, torn down your altars, and put your prophets to death with the sword. I am the only one left, and now they are trying to kill me too."

➜ **THINK** Elijah tells God he's down. Really down. Twice. Do you think God sounds ready to spew anger at Elijah for how he feels? Explain.

How does God respond? What's all that shake, rattle, and roll supposed to prove?

Rocks shatter. The earth shakes. The mountain burns. God, however, doesn't show up in any of those spectacular demonstrations of power. He instead comes to Elijah in calmness, "a gentle whisper," or what the King James Version of the Bible famously calls a "still small voice." God comes to soothe Elijah, not scream at him. That whisper means "Trust me!"

➜ **LIVE** When has being a Christian made you feel *more* lonely— not less?

Why talk to God when you feel alone? What kind of help can you expect from him?

In the next verses of this passage, God says he has a pack of likeminded friends for Elijah—7000, to be exact, "all whose knees have not bowed down to Baal" (1 Kings 19:18). God also gives the prophet a serious spiritual partner named Elisha (1 Kings 19:19).

How do you expect God to fix a lonely situation? What do you think he expects you to do?

➜   **WRAP** You might assume that following Jesus will give you more than enough merry friendships. It should. But when it doesn't, talk to God. Look patiently for his answers. And do your part. God had a mob of friends for Elijah, but he instructed the prophet to ditch his dark thoughts, go home, and track them down. Elijah didn't experience God's cure for his misery until he talked straight-up with God and let the Lord lead him to other loyal followers.

»   MORE THOUGHTS TO MULL

- Has God ever provided you with friends you didn't expect? What happened?

- Have you ever felt lonely even while surrounded by friends—maybe even a swarm of Christian friends?

- Ask God for help when you feel lonely. If you rarely feel lonely, then ask God to help you meet the needs of someone who does.

» MORE SCRIPTURES TO DIG

- Elijah has been doing God's work for many years, but God doesn't ship Elijah off to retirement in some palm-lined oasis. Instead, God sends him back where he came from. But God also radically rearranges Elijah's situation. Elijah is to install a new king in Aram—a nation that's constantly at war with Israel. And he also gets to declare a new king over Israel—to replace the wicked queen who's hunting him. That's the rapid-fire action of **1 Kings 19:15-17**. If Elijah hadn't followed God's command to head back home, he never would have experienced God's amazing answers to his groanings, including his new friendship with Elisha in **1 Kings 19:18-21**.

- Don't miss the highs and lows of this whole scene. Flip back to **1 Kings 18:1-46** to spot Elijah's spectacular clash with the prophets of that fake god, Baal. In **1 Kings 19:1-4** you see his run-in with the bloodthirsty queen Jezebel. And you can see how the rest of the story wraps up in **1 Kings 19:5-21**.

- The prophet Elisha is just one of 7000 faithful-to-God friends Elijah didn't even know about. After God snatched Elijah to heaven in **2 Kings 2**, Elisha took over his mentor's job as God's leading spokesperson. Look in **2 Kings 1–13** for Elisha's story.

- Take time to review God's major facts about major friends by rereading a few of the big passages featured at the start of this book: **1 John 4:7-12, 19-21**; **Hebrews 10:24-25**; and **2 Timothy 2:22**.

20. NEVER ALONE

God is your faithful friend

Psalm 27:1

The Lord is my light and my salvation—whom shall I fear? The Lord is the stronghold of my life—of whom shall I be afraid?

➔ **START** When your social studies teacher jets your class to a lush tropical island for your unit on "The Organization of Human Societies," you figure you're in for some fun. When you learn you'll need to eat bugs to survive—and that you'll all get to vote the unpopular people off the island—you wonder how you'll do. But when you're the first person your classmates eject from your tribal society, you wish you'd been shipwrecked all by your lonesome on your own speck of an island.

How do you react—thoughts, words, and actions—when your enemies behave badly and your friends act even worse?

➔ **READ** Psalm 27:1-5

¹The Lord is my light and my salvation—whom shall I fear? The Lord is the stronghold of my life—of whom shall I be afraid? ²When the wicked advance against me to devour me, it is my enemies and my foes who will stumble and fall. ³Though an army besiege me, my heart will not fear; though war break out against me, even then I will be confident. ⁴One thing I ask from the Lord, this only do I seek: that I may dwell in the house of the Lord all the days of my life, to gaze on the beauty of the Lord and to seek him in his temple. ⁵For in the day of trouble he will keep me safe in his dwelling; he will hide me in the shelter of his tabernacle and set me high upon a rock.

➔ **THINK** These amazing words spill from the mouth of David, the most fabulous and famous king of God's ancient Old Testament people. Try to track his reasoning: You've got God on your side—who or what is left to fear?

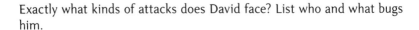

Exactly what kinds of attacks does David face? List who and what bugs him.

In the midst of those crushing troubles, what does David request from God? Why ask for that?

You'd think David would beg God for a fleet of tanks and Humvees. Yet he trusts God to keep him safe in "the house of the Lord." At that point, before the temple is built, God's house is a mere tent where Israel gathers to worship (2 Samuel 7:1-2). David doesn't look for safety in a fort. He flees to God's presence.

➜   **LIVE** Suppose you were abandoned by every friend you ever had. How does God figure into your plans—or not?

Look back at David's prayer. Remind yourself of what he asked for. It's the most crucial request you can utter when human friends leave you lonely. Use your own words to write a prayer like David's:

What other kinds of help can you ask God for? What are you going to do while you wait for God's answers?

➜ **WRAP** God is your tightest friend when all of life goes swell. Yet even on days when you want to crawl away and curl up in a ball, you're never alone. God is your ultimate Friend, the one Being in the universe who will never let you go.

» MORE THOUGHTS TO MULL

- Why do you think God sometimes allows us to feel as though every human friend has ditched us?

- When have you most needed God to survive?

- What do you need from God right now to help you survive and thrive in life? Talk to him about it.

» MORE SCRIPTURES TO DIG

- Look at **Psalm 27:13-14**. When does David expect God's help to show up? What's he going to do in the meantime?

- David is tough enough to survive some of life's harshest attacks. As a teenage shepherd, he kills lions and bears that are trying to maul his sheep (**1 Samuel 17:36**). As a young guy, he dodges spears hurled by an insane king (**1 Samuel 18:10-11**). And as an adult, he becomes a fearsome warrior and king (**2 Samuel 5:3-5**). But when the whole world gangs up on him, he doesn't depend on his own smarts to survive. He relies on God. You might not like to admit that you ever feel lonely, but David knows that being alone is part of life. He knows when he needs help.

- Flip to **Matthew 28:20** and **Hebrews 13:5-6**, where God promises to never leave you.

- Read **Psalm 84** for more about the total safety of sticking close to God. And when you're feeling completely isolated, check **Psalm 73:21-28**. Some days you might feel as though life has left you with no support. Yet there's one fact you can cling to: No matter what, you've always got God—and he's always got you.

Many people think teenagers aren't capable of much. But Zach Hunter is proving those people wrong. He's only fifteen, but he's working to end slavery in the world—and he's making changes that affect millions of people. Find out how Zach is making a difference and how you can make changes in the things that you see wrong with our world.

Be the Change
Your Guide to Freeing Slaves and Changing the World
Zach Hunter
RETAIL $9.99
ISBN 0-310-27756-6

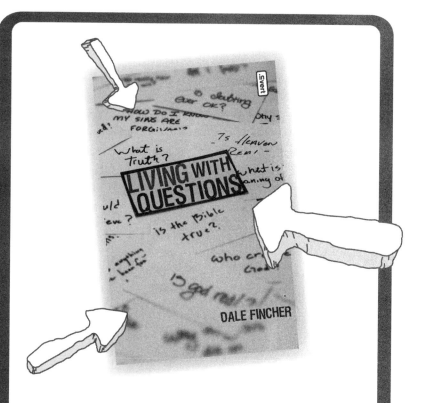

If you've ever wondered if God is really there and listening, if you're good enough, or what's so great about heaven, you're not alone. We all have had personal questions, but the answers are often harder to come by. In this book, you'll discover how to navigate your big questions, and what the answers mean for your life and faith.

Living with Questions
Dale Fincher
RETAIL $9.99
ISBN 0-310-27664-0

Love This! contains real-life stories of people like you who've found ways to love their neighbors. It will challenge you to make a difference in your world by loving people who are often ignored or unloved—the homeless, the addicted, the elderly, those of different races, even your enemies—and show you tangible ways you can demonstrate that love.

Love This!
Learning to Make It a Way of Life, Not Just a Word
Andy Braner
RETAIL $12.99
ISBN 0-310-27380-3

Visit www.invertbooks.com or your local bookstore.